Bridging Boundaries: Love and Inter-Caste Marriages in the Indian Subcontinent

C. P. Kumar

Reiki Healer

Roorkee - 247667, India

Disclaimer

While every effort has been made to ensure the accuracy and completeness of the content in this book, the author cannot guarantee that the information contained herein is error-free, up-to-date, or suitable for every individual circumstance.

The author shall not be held liable or responsible for any errors or omissions in the content of the book, nor for any damages, or losses that may arise from any actions taken based upon the suggestions or contents presented in the book.

Readers are advised to use their own judgment and discretion in applying the information provided in this book, and to consult with qualified professionals before taking any action based on the contents of this book. The author disclaims any and all liability or responsibility for any actions taken or not taken based on the information contained in this book.

DEDICATION

To all those who believe in the power of love and the strength of human connection, this book is dedicated to you. It is dedicated to the individuals who have dared to cross the boundaries of caste, challenging social norms and traditional conventions.

To the couples who have embraced love as the guiding force in their lives, navigating through the complexities of inter-caste marriages, we honor your resilience and determination. This book is dedicated to you, for your unwavering commitment to building bridges between communities and fostering understanding.

To the trailblazers who have fought against the constraints of societal expectations, striving to reshape social hierarchies and create a more inclusive society, we acknowledge your courage and perseverance. This dedication is a tribute to your relentless pursuit of equality and justice.

To the families who have experienced the transformative power of love marriages, and have witnessed firsthand the challenges and joys that come with breaking the barriers of tradition, we recognize your strength and adaptability. This dedication is for you, as you navigate the ever-evolving dynamics within your own households.

To the activists, scholars, and policymakers who have devoted their lives to advocating for the rights of individuals in love and inter-caste marriages, we express our gratitude for your tireless efforts. This dedication serves as a reminder of the importance of your work in shaping a more progressive and inclusive society.

Lastly, to the future generations who will inherit the legacy of love and inter-caste marriages, may this book provide you with insights, knowledge, and inspiration. It is dedicated to your dreams of a more harmonious and accepting world.

May this exploration of love and inter-caste marriages in the Indian subcontinent serve as a testament to the power of love, the strength of unity, and the limitless potential of human connections.

C. P. Kumar

CONTENTS

PREFACE

This book explores the intricate and evolving landscape of love and inter-caste marriages in the Indian subcontinent. It delves into the historical perspective, sociocultural factors, legal aspects, socioeconomic implications, family dynamics, and gender roles surrounding these unions.

By examining the contrast between love and arranged marriages, this book offers a comparative analysis to understand their unique dynamics in the Indian context. It also delves into the challenges and transformative potential of inter-caste marriages in breaking social barriers and reshaping social hierarchies.

The book explores the psychological and emotional dimensions of love marriages, along with the legal framework that governs these unions. It analyzes the socioeconomic impact of love and inter-caste marriages and their influence on family dynamics.

Addressing the darker side, it discusses issues of honor killings and violence, highlighting the need for acceptance and change. The book also explores the impact of these marriages on gender roles, gender equality, and the generation gap in attitudes towards them.

Considering the urban-rural divide and the role of media in shaping perceptions, the book examines variations in experiences and challenges faced by couples in different settings. Finally, it contemplates future trends and prospects for love and inter-caste marriages in the Indian subcontinent, inspiring conversations and actions for inclusivity and understanding.

"Bridging Boundaries: Love and Inter-Caste Marriages in the Indian Subcontinent" aims to illuminate the multifaceted dimensions of these unions, foster empathy, encourage dialogue, and contribute to transforming societal attitudes and norms.

C. P. Kumar
Reiki Healer
Former Scientist 'G', National Institute of Hydrology
Roorkee - 247667, India
E-mail: cpkumar@yahoo.com
Web: https://www.angelfire.com/nh/cpkumar/virgo.html

Chapter 1. Introduction to Love Marriages and Inter-caste Marriages

Introduction

Love and marriage have always been intertwined, forming the foundation of human relationships throughout history. In the Indian subcontinent, where tradition and cultural norms hold significant influence, love marriages and inter-caste marriages have emerged as powerful catalysts for change. These unions challenge long-standing societal boundaries and provide a platform for individuals to transcend the limitations imposed by caste, class, and religion. This article serves as an introduction to the complex dynamics of love marriages and inter-caste marriages, highlighting their significance in the context of the Indian subcontinent.

Love Marriages: Defying Social Conventions

1. The Evolution of Love Marriages

Love marriages, characterized by individuals choosing their life partners based on affection and personal compatibility, have seen a gradual transformation in the Indian subcontinent. Historically, arranged marriages were the dominant practice, where families played a pivotal role in selecting suitable partners for their children. However, with the advent of modernization, urbanization, and exposure to diverse cultures, the concept of love marriages gained prominence.

2. Factors Influencing Love Marriages

Several factors have contributed to the rise of love marriages. The increasing levels of education and economic independence among men and women have empowered individuals to make autonomous decisions regarding their life partners. Exposure to Western ideals through media, globalization, and the internet has also played a crucial role in shaping the mindset of the younger generation, fostering a more individualistic approach to love and relationships.

3. Challenges and Benefits of Love Marriages

Love marriages are not devoid of challenges. Couples often face opposition from conservative families who adhere strictly to traditional values and societal norms. However, love marriages offer unique advantages, such as the opportunity for individuals to choose partners based on shared interests, emotional compatibility, and mutual understanding. This can lead to stronger marital bonds and a sense of personal fulfillment.

Inter-caste Marriages: Breaking Barriers

1. The Significance of Caste in Indian Society

Caste has long been a deeply ingrained social institution in the Indian subcontinent, determining social hierarchy, occupation, and marital alliances. The caste system has created divisions and prejudices, making inter-caste marriages a bold and transformative act.

2. The Changing Landscape of Inter-caste Marriages

Inter-caste marriages challenge the traditional caste-based system by bringing together individuals from different social backgrounds. They provide an opportunity to break down stereotypes, foster inclusivity, and promote social harmony. In recent years, there has been a notable increase in inter-caste marriages, signaling a shift towards a more egalitarian society.

3. Overcoming Obstacles in Inter-caste Marriages

Inter-caste marriages often face significant obstacles, including societal pressure, family disapproval, and legal challenges. These unions require couples to navigate through complex dynamics and societal prejudices. However, inter-caste marriages also offer the potential for social transformation, as they challenge deep-rooted prejudices and contribute to the dismantling of the caste system.

Bridging Boundaries: Love and Inter-caste Marriages in the Indian Subcontinent

1. Social Impact of Love and Inter-caste Marriages

Love marriages and inter-caste marriages have far-reaching social implications. They serve as a catalyst for social change, promoting equality, individual freedom, and inclusivity. By challenging traditional norms and expectations, these marriages pave the way for a more progressive and inclusive society.

2. Legal Perspective and Policy Reforms

The legal landscape surrounding love marriages and inter-caste marriages has undergone significant changes in recent years. Legal reforms have aimed to protect the rights of individuals to choose their life partners freely, irrespective of caste, religion, or gender. These reforms have provided legal support and safeguards for couples, encouraging the practice of love and inter-caste marriages.

3. The Role of Education and Awareness

Education and awareness play a crucial role in fostering acceptance and understanding of love and inter-caste marriages. By promoting inclusivity and challenging discriminatory beliefs, educational institutions, media platforms, and social organizations can contribute to changing societal attitudes and eliminating biases against these marriages.

Conclusion

Love marriages and inter-caste marriages have emerged as powerful agents of change, bridging boundaries and challenging the traditional social fabric in the Indian subcontinent. These unions offer individuals the opportunity to break free from societal constraints, choose their life partners based on love and compatibility, and promote a more inclusive and egalitarian society. Understanding the complexities and significance of love marriages and inter-caste marriages is essential to fostering social transformation and creating a future that embraces diversity and love.

Introduction

Marriage is a significant institution in the Indian subcontinent, deeply rooted in its rich cultural and historical heritage. Over the centuries, the region has witnessed a fascinating evolution of marriage patterns, influenced by various factors such as religion, caste, class, and social norms. This article explores the historical perspective of marriage in the Indian subcontinent, tracing the changing trends and shedding light on the phenomenon of inter-caste marriages.

Early Vedic Period: Rituals and Arranged Marriages

In the ancient times of the Vedic period, marriages were considered sacraments and held great religious significance. The rituals and ceremonies associated with marriage were elaborately detailed in the sacred texts, emphasizing the importance of solemnizing the union within one's own caste. During this era, marriage was primarily an arranged affair, with families playing a crucial role in the selection of spouses.

Classical Era: Dynastic Alliances and Social Hierarchy

As the Indian subcontinent progressed into the classical era, the institution of marriage began to serve not only as a means of social union but also as a tool for political alliances. Dynastic marriages were commonly used to strengthen political ties and forge alliances between kingdoms. Marriages within one's own caste and social hierarchy were still prevalent during this period, as inter-caste marriages were often seen as a threat to social order.

Medieval Period: Influence of Islam and Sufism

With the arrival of Islam in the Indian subcontinent during the medieval period, marriage patterns underwent significant transformations. Islamic teachings brought forth the concept of monogamy and emphasized the equality of spouses in marriage. Sufi saints and their followers further propagated the idea of love and devotion as essential elements of a marital relationship. However, the practice of endogamy and the preference for marriages within one's own caste continued to dominate society.

Colonial Era: Interactions and Changing Dynamics

The arrival of European colonial powers in the Indian subcontinent during the 16th century brought about significant changes in marriage patterns. The British, in particular, had a profound impact on the social structure of the region. British colonial rule introduced western concepts of individualism, personal choice, and romantic love. These influences gradually led to a shift in societal attitudes towards marriage.

Independence and Modernization: Inter-Caste Marriages as a Social Movement

Following India's independence in 1947, the country witnessed a wave of social reforms and modernization. Inter-caste marriages emerged as a social movement, challenging traditional norms and caste-based discrimination. The Constitution of India, enacted in 1950, outlawed untouchability and promoted the principle of equality among citizens. This constitutional guarantee provided impetus to individuals seeking to break barriers and marry outside their caste.

Contemporary Scenario: Love and Inter-Caste Marriages

In recent years, inter-caste marriages have gained further acceptance and recognition in the Indian subcontinent. The younger generation, more exposed to globalization and influenced by progressive ideas, is increasingly opting for love marriages and inter-caste unions. The rise of education, urbanization, and economic independence has played a significant role in dismantling caste barriers and fostering inter-caste marriages.

Conclusion

The evolution of marriage patterns in the Indian subcontinent reflects the complex interplay of cultural, religious, and societal factors. From the early Vedic period to the present day, the institution of marriage has witnessed remarkable transformations. While arranged marriages and caste considerations were dominant in the past, inter-caste marriages have gradually emerged as a symbol of social progress and individual choice.

Chapter 3. Sociocultural Factors Influencing Love Marriages and Inter-caste Marriages

Introduction

Love marriages and inter-caste marriages have become increasingly prevalent in the Indian subcontinent, challenging long-standing societal norms and traditions. In this article, we explore the sociocultural factors that influence these types of marriages and their significance in bridging boundaries within the region. By examining the evolving perspectives and changing dynamics, we aim to shed light on the complexities and impact of love and inter-caste marriages.

Traditional Arranged Marriages and Social Expectations

Arranged marriages have been deeply ingrained in the cultural fabric of the Indian subcontinent. The strong emphasis on family honor, community values, and social expectations often shape the choice of a spouse. Traditional beliefs uphold the importance of marrying within one's own caste, religion, or social class, reinforcing the barriers to love and inter-caste marriages.

Influence of Changing Attitudes

However, in recent years, there has been a significant shift in attitudes towards marriage. Modernization, globalization, and exposure to different cultures have influenced the younger generation, leading to a transformation in their outlook on love and marriage. Young adults are increasingly prioritizing personal happiness, emotional compatibility, and mutual respect over traditional considerations, challenging societal norms and paving the way for love marriages.

Love Marriages: Breaking the Mold

Love marriages, based on emotional attachment and personal choice, transcend the boundaries set by caste, religion, and social class. This emerging trend signifies a departure from the traditional mindset, giving individuals the freedom to choose their life partners based on love, shared values, and compatibility. The growing acceptance of love marriages is slowly dismantling the barriers created by the caste system and fostering a more inclusive society.

Inter-caste Marriages: Fostering Social Integration

Inter-caste marriages go a step further in challenging social boundaries, as they involve individuals from different castes or sub-castes. These unions have the potential to promote social integration, dismantle caste-based discrimination, and foster a sense of unity. Inter-caste marriages challenge the deep-rooted prejudices and biases associated with caste, encouraging communities to break free from rigid social hierarchies and embrace inclusivity.

Impact on Gender Roles and Women's Empowerment

Love and inter-caste marriages have also had a significant impact on gender roles and women's empowerment in the Indian subcontinent. By choosing their partners based on love and compatibility, individuals are breaking away from the patriarchal tradition of arranged marriages, where decisions are often made by parents or elders. Love marriages provide women with greater agency in choosing their life partners, thereby empowering them to challenge societal norms and pursue their aspirations.

Parental Opposition and Societal Challenges

Despite the increasing acceptance of love and inter-caste marriages, many couples still face opposition from their families and society at large. Traditional mindsets, fear of social stigma, concerns about preserving family honor, and the perceived threat to caste endogamy often contribute to this opposition. Such challenges highlight the need for increased awareness, dialogue, and sensitization to foster understanding and acceptance of diverse marital choices.

Legal and Policy Frameworks

The legal and policy frameworks in the Indian subcontinent have also played a role in shaping the landscape of love and inter-caste marriages. Legislative changes and court judgments, such as the Special Marriage Act and landmark judgments supporting inter-caste marriages, have provided legal protection and recognition to couples. These measures have been instrumental in strengthening the rights of individuals and promoting social inclusivity.

Social Activism and Awareness Campaigns

Social activism and awareness campaigns have been pivotal in challenging social biases and advocating for the rights of couples in love and inter-caste marriages. Non-governmental organizations, support groups, and online platforms have emerged as safe spaces for couples to share their experiences, seek guidance, and garner support. These initiatives play a crucial role in changing mindsets, promoting acceptance, and bridging societal boundaries.

Conclusion

Love marriages and inter-caste marriages are redefining the social landscape of the Indian subcontinent. By challenging long-standing traditions and breaking social barriers, these unions hold the potential to foster inclusivity, social integration, and gender equality. However, despite the progress made, there is still work to be done to ensure widespread acceptance and support for couples choosing love and inter-caste marriages. Bridging boundaries in love and inter-caste marriages requires collective efforts from individuals, families, communities, and society as a whole.

Chapter 4. Love vs. Arranged Marriages
A Comparative Analysis

Introduction

Marriage is a significant institution that binds individuals together in a lifelong commitment. In the Indian subcontinent, marriage holds immense cultural and social importance. Traditionally, two primary approaches to marriage prevail: love marriages and arranged marriages. This article aims to provide a comparative analysis of these two types of marriages, focusing on their origins, cultural contexts, advantages, disadvantages, and their impact on inter-caste marriages in the Indian subcontinent.

Love Marriages

Love marriages are based on the foundation of romantic attraction and emotional compatibility between two individuals. In this type of marriage, the individuals involved make the choice of their life partner independently. Love marriages are relatively modern phenomena, influenced by Western ideals of individualism and personal choice. They emphasize the importance of love and personal happiness in marriage.

1. Origins and Cultural Context

Love marriages find their roots in societies where individual freedom and personal choice are highly valued. In Western cultures, romantic love has been a driving force behind marital unions for centuries. However, in the Indian subcontinent, love marriages were uncommon until recent times due to the prevalence of arranged marriages deeply rooted in tradition and societal norms.

2. Advantages

One of the primary advantages of love marriages is the freedom of choice. Individuals have the opportunity to select their life partner based on their personal preferences, compatibility, and shared values. Love marriages are often seen as a union of equals, where both partners have a say in decision-making processes. Additionally, love marriages may foster a deeper understanding and emotional bond between the couple as they embark on their marital journey.

3. Disadvantages

Despite the advantages, love marriages are not without challenges. One of the significant concerns is the potential clash between families when the choice of partner does not align with societal expectations or caste considerations. Inter-caste marriages, in particular, face societal resistance due to deeply ingrained caste prejudices. Moreover, love marriages may place an immense emotional burden on the individuals involved, as they have to navigate through societal pressure and familial disapproval.

Arranged Marriages

Arranged marriages are prevalent in many cultures, including India, where they have been the dominant form of marital union for centuries. In this type of marriage, families take the lead in selecting a suitable partner for their children based on factors such as caste, social standing, and compatibility of families. Arranged marriages prioritize the harmony and stability of the union, often considering practical considerations over romantic love.

1. Origins and Cultural Context

Arranged marriages have deep historical roots in the Indian subcontinent, influenced by cultural, religious, and social norms. The practice of arranged marriages is grounded in the belief that families are better equipped to make decisions that ensure long-term compatibility, financial stability, and social cohesion. It is seen as a union not just between two individuals but between families as well.

2. Advantages

One of the primary advantages of arranged marriages is the involvement of families in the decision-making process. Families play a vital role in assessing the compatibility of the potential partners, considering factors beyond romantic attraction. Arranged marriages also tend to have a higher success rate due to the emphasis on shared values, common backgrounds, and mutual understanding. Additionally, arranged marriages often receive strong support from extended family networks, providing a broader support system for the couple.

3. Disadvantages

Despite the benefits, arranged marriages face criticisms and challenges. One of the significant criticisms is the limited personal agency for the individuals involved, as they have limited say in selecting their life partner. Arranged marriages can sometimes lead to a lack of emotional compatibility or understanding between partners who may have had limited interactions before marriage. Additionally, the pressure to conform to societal and familial expectations may result in compromised personal happiness.

Love vs. Arranged Marriages: Impact on Inter-Caste Marriages

Inter-caste marriages, which involve individuals from different castes, have long been a topic of discussion in the Indian subcontinent. Both love and arranged marriages have varying impacts on inter-caste marriages.

1. Love Marriages

Love marriages have been instrumental in breaking down caste barriers and promoting inter-caste unions. When individuals choose their life partners based on love and compatibility, they often transcend caste boundaries. Love marriages challenge traditional norms and foster social integration by promoting inter-caste marriages, leading to the possibility of a more egalitarian society.

2. Arranged Marriages

In contrast, arranged marriages have historically adhered to caste considerations, perpetuating the caste system. Families often prioritize preserving social status, caste purity, and familial honor in the selection of a partner. However, there is a gradual shift in mindset, and arranged marriages are now witnessing an increasing number of inter-caste unions, driven by evolving societal values and the influence of modern education.

Conclusion

Love marriages and arranged marriages are two distinct approaches to marital unions, each with its own set of advantages and disadvantages. While love marriages prioritize personal choice and emotional compatibility, arranged marriages emphasize practical considerations and familial harmony. Both types of marriages have unique cultural contexts and implications for inter-caste marriages in the Indian subcontinent. As societal attitudes continue to evolve, a balance between personal choice and societal expectations can lead to a more inclusive and progressive approach to marriage, bridging the boundaries between love and arranged unions in the Indian subcontinent.

Introduction

Love knows no boundaries. It transcends societal constructs, cultural barriers, and even the rigid divisions of caste. Inter-caste marriages, once considered taboo in the Indian subcontinent, are now emerging as a symbol of social progress and a powerful force for change. In this article, we delve into the significance of inter-caste marriages, explore the challenges they face, and celebrate the couples who are courageously challenging age-old norms to build a more inclusive society.

The Legacy of Caste Divisions

India's caste system, deeply ingrained in society for centuries, has perpetuated social hierarchies and divisions. Marriages within one's caste were traditionally encouraged, serving to preserve the social order. This practice restricted individuals from freely choosing their life partners, reinforcing caste-based discrimination and inequality.

Winds of Change

Over the years, the Indian subcontinent has witnessed a remarkable shift in societal attitudes towards inter-caste marriages. This transformation can be attributed to several factors, including increased education and exposure to diverse cultures, urbanization, and the influence of media. Younger generations are challenging the status quo, embracing love across caste lines, and paving the way for a more inclusive society.

Breaking Stereotypes

Inter-caste marriages serve as a catalyst for dismantling stereotypes and dispelling prejudice. When couples from different castes choose to unite in matrimony, they shatter long-held beliefs about the inherent superiority or inferiority of particular castes. These unions challenge rigid notions of purity and impurity, emphasizing the fundamental equality of all individuals.

Strengthening Social Cohesion

Inter-caste marriages have the power to foster social cohesion by bridging gaps between communities. As couples from diverse castes come together, they create extended networks of families and friends that transcend caste lines. These connections promote cross-cultural understanding, empathy, and cooperation, helping to erode caste-based prejudices and foster a sense of unity among communities.

Empowering Individuals

For individuals in inter-caste marriages, love becomes a transformative force. By defying societal expectations, they assert their agency and reclaim the right to choose their life partners based on love and compatibility, rather than caste. These unions empower individuals to challenge oppressive social norms and create their own narratives, contributing to their personal growth and self-realization.

The Role of Legislation

Legal measures have played a significant role in facilitating inter-caste marriages and protecting the rights of couples. The Special Marriage Act, enacted in India, allows individuals from different castes to marry and register their unions irrespective of their caste or religion. Such legal provisions offer a crucial framework for couples to solemnize their relationships and safeguard their rights.

Navigating Challenges

Despite the progress made, inter-caste marriages still face challenges and resistance from conservative sections of society. Families may object, citing concerns about cultural compatibility, societal backlash, or the preservation of caste identity. Couples often endure societal scrutiny, prejudice, and discrimination. However, their resilience and determination are gradually transforming mindsets and paving the way for a more inclusive future.

Celebrating Love Across Caste Lines

While the journey of inter-caste couples may be arduous, it is essential to celebrate their courage and resilience. Their love stories are testaments to the power of love to transcend social barriers and foster understanding. By sharing their experiences and triumphs, these couples inspire others, challenging the regressive norms that impede social progress.

Conclusion

Inter-caste marriages are catalysts for social change in the Indian subcontinent. They challenge long-standing social norms, break down stereotypes, and promote inclusivity. The increasing acceptance of inter-caste marriages signifies a shift towards a more egalitarian society, where love triumphs over division. As we celebrate the stories of inter-caste couples, let us recognize their invaluable contribution to building a future free from the shackles of caste-based discrimination, and where love knows no boundaries.

Introduction

Love and marriage are deeply intertwined in the fabric of Indian society. For centuries, arranged marriages have been the traditional norm, with families playing a significant role in choosing life partners. However, over the past few decades, love marriages have gained prominence, challenging the long-established customs and bridging societal boundaries. This article delves into the realm of love marriages in the Indian context, shedding light on the dynamics, challenges, and evolving perspectives surrounding romantic relationships.

Historical Perspectives on Indian Marriages

In order to understand the significance of love marriages in India, it is essential to explore the historical context of Indian marriages. Traditional arranged marriages were influenced by factors such as caste, religion, and social standing. Marriage was often seen as an alliance between families, rather than a union of individuals driven by romantic love. This backdrop laid the foundation for the emergence of love marriages as an alternative approach.

The Rise of Love Marriages

1. Cultural Shifts and Changing Mindsets

Love marriages have gained momentum due to various cultural shifts in Indian society. The influence of western media, increased exposure to diverse cultures, and the rise of individualism have played pivotal roles in altering traditional marriage practices. Younger generations are increasingly seeking companionship based on compatibility, shared interests, and emotional connection, rather than purely relying on familial considerations.

2. Urbanization and Education

Rapid urbanization and the expansion of education have been instrumental in fostering love marriages. As young individuals move away from their hometowns for education and employment opportunities, they come into contact with diverse communities and people. These experiences create avenues for cross-cultural interactions and the formation of romantic relationships outside the boundaries of caste and religion.

Inter-Caste Love Marriages

1. Breaking the Shackles of Caste

Inter-caste love marriages challenge the deeply ingrained caste system in India. Such unions defy societal norms and prejudices, as individuals choose their life partners based on love rather than caste considerations. Inter-caste love marriages have become a catalyst for social change, breaking down barriers and fostering greater acceptance of diversity.

2. Struggles and Triumphs

Inter-caste love marriages often face resistance from families, societal disapproval, and even violence in some cases. The couples must navigate through these challenges, exhibiting immense strength and resilience. However, their triumphs in the face of adversity inspire others to challenge societal norms and embrace love beyond caste boundaries.

The Role of Gender

1. Empowerment of Women

Love marriages have emerged as a powerful tool for women's empowerment in the Indian context. By choosing their life partners based on love, women assert their agency and challenge traditional gender roles. Love marriages provide them with a platform to break free from societal expectations and pursue personal happiness.

2. Honor Killings and Legal Reforms

Love marriages, particularly inter-caste marriages, have unfortunately been marred by instances of honor killings. The deeply rooted notion of preserving family honor often leads to tragic consequences. However, these incidents have spurred legal reforms, with stringent laws being enacted to curb such violence and protect couples who choose love over societal norms.

The Changing Landscape and Future Perspectives

1. Acceptance and Transformation

With each passing generation, love marriages are gaining wider acceptance in Indian society. Although certain conservative mindsets still resist this change, there is a gradual shift towards embracing individual choice and romantic relationships. Love marriages are transforming the social fabric, fostering a society that values personal happiness and emotional well-being.

2. Cultural Exchange and Hybrid Identities

Love marriages often result in cultural exchange and the creation of hybrid identities. When individuals from diverse backgrounds come together in love, they not only bridge the boundaries of caste and religion but also create a unique blend of traditions, beliefs, and practices. This cultural fusion enriches the Indian subcontinent, fostering a sense of unity in diversity.

Conclusion

Love marriages are a testament to the power of love, breaking societal barriers and bridging boundaries in the Indian context. As more individuals choose their life partners based on love and compatibility, rather than societal expectations, the landscape of Indian marriages continues to evolve. Love marriages pave the way for a more inclusive and progressive society, where individual happiness and emotional fulfillment take precedence over rigid customs and traditions. By embracing love across caste, religion, and social boundaries, India embraces a future that celebrates unity, diversity, and personal freedom.

Introduction

Marriage is a sacred union that transcends boundaries of caste, religion, and social status. In the Indian subcontinent, inter-caste marriages have emerged as a significant phenomenon that challenges traditional social norms. This article explores the legal aspects surrounding inter-caste marriages in the context of marriage laws in India. It aims to shed light on the evolution of these laws, the rights of individuals entering into inter-caste marriages, and the role of legislation in promoting social integration and inclusivity.

Historical Background

Inter-caste marriages have been a subject of societal debate in India for centuries. Caste-based discrimination and social taboos have often hindered such unions. However, with the passage of time, societal attitudes have evolved, and legal frameworks have been established to address the concerns surrounding inter-caste marriages.

The Special Marriage Act, 1954

The Special Marriage Act, 1954 is a key legislative enactment in India that facilitates inter-caste marriages. This Act allows individuals from different castes, religions, or communities to solemnize their marriage without the need for religious conversion. It provides a legal framework for inter-caste marriages, ensuring the rights and protection of the individuals involved.

Consent and Age

One of the fundamental requirements for a valid marriage is the free and informed consent of both parties. The legal age for marriage in India is 18 years for females and 21 years for males. Regardless of caste, inter-caste marriages must adhere to these age requirements and ensure that both parties enter the union willingly and without coercion.

Rights and Benefits

Inter-caste marriages enjoy the same legal recognition and benefits as any other marriage. The rights and benefits include inheritance, property rights, child custody, and the right to maintenance. The legal framework ensures that these rights are protected irrespective of caste or community.

Legal Challenges and Protection

Despite the legal provisions, inter-caste marriages often face societal and familial opposition. In some cases, couples may face threats, harassment, or violence from their families or communities. The law provides protection to such individuals through various mechanisms, including restraining orders, police assistance, and legal remedies.

Legal Safeguards

To further protect individuals in inter-caste marriages, the law incorporates specific provisions. These safeguards aim to prevent coercion, fraud, or undue influence in the marriage process. The presence of witnesses during the marriage ceremony and the requirement of registration within a specific time frame are among the safeguards established by the law.

Social Impact and Changing Attitudes

Inter-caste marriages play a crucial role in breaking down barriers and fostering social integration. They challenge deeply entrenched notions of caste-based discrimination and promote inclusivity and equality. With time, society's attitude towards inter-caste marriages is gradually evolving, contributing to a more tolerant and inclusive society.

Role of Education and Awareness

Promoting education and awareness about inter-caste marriages and their legal aspects is essential. Educating individuals about their rights, legal safeguards, and the social implications of inter-caste marriages can empower them to make informed decisions and navigate societal challenges.

Conclusion

Inter-caste marriages represent a significant shift in societal norms and are reshaping the Indian subcontinent's social fabric. The legal framework surrounding inter-caste marriages, as embodied by the Special Marriage Act, ensures the protection of individuals and their rights. While challenges and social prejudices persist, education and awareness can contribute to a more inclusive and harmonious society that embraces love and inter-caste marriages.

Chapter 8. Socioeconomic Implications of Love and Inter-caste Marriages

Introduction

Love and inter-caste marriages have long been a topic of discussion and debate, particularly in the Indian subcontinent. These unions challenge traditional societal norms, as they involve individuals from different castes coming together in matrimony. Beyond the emotional and personal dimensions, such marriages also have significant socioeconomic implications. This article explores the various socioeconomic factors that are influenced by love and inter-caste marriages, shedding light on both the positive and negative aspects of these unions.

Challenging Caste-Based Social Hierarchies

Inter-caste marriages break down the rigid caste system, which has historically divided Indian society. By choosing partners from different castes, individuals challenge the deeply entrenched social hierarchies and bring about a more egalitarian society. Love marriages, regardless of caste, encourage a shift towards meritocracy, where compatibility and personal qualities take precedence over birth-based categorizations. This shift can potentially lead to the dismantling of caste-based discrimination and foster a more inclusive society.

Redefining Cultural Identity

Inter-caste marriages provide an opportunity for individuals to redefine their cultural identity. When two people from different castes come together, they often blend their cultural practices and traditions, creating a unique fusion of customs. This amalgamation allows for the preservation of diverse cultural heritage while simultaneously fostering a sense of unity and understanding. Children born out of such marriages inherit a rich multicultural background, which can empower them to embrace diversity and contribute to a pluralistic society.

Economic Mobility

Inter-caste marriages can have a positive impact on economic mobility for individuals and families involved. By choosing their partners based on personal compatibility rather than caste-based considerations, individuals open themselves up to a wider pool of potential partners. This often leads to the selection of partners who may have different socioeconomic backgrounds, educational qualifications, or professional aspirations. Consequently, inter-caste marriages can promote upward mobility, enabling individuals to access new opportunities and resources that may have been otherwise inaccessible due to the constraints of their own caste.

Bridging Economic Disparities

Inter-caste marriages can play a role in bridging economic disparities that exist within society. As individuals from different castes unite, their families may pool resources and share economic burdens, leading to an equitable distribution of wealth. This can help alleviate financial strain and provide a more stable foundation for future generations. Additionally, inter-caste marriages can foster economic interdependence between different castes, thereby promoting economic cooperation and reducing disparities in wealth and income.

Social Integration and Cohesion

Love and inter-caste marriages contribute to social integration by fostering connections between different castes. As families from diverse backgrounds come together, they create networks of relationships that transcend traditional caste boundaries. These connections promote social cohesion, mutual understanding, and empathy, breaking down prejudices and stereotypes associated with specific castes. Inter-caste marriages can play a vital role in building bridges and nurturing a sense of unity and shared destiny within the larger society.

Resistance and Backlash

While love and inter-caste marriages bring about numerous positive changes, they also face resistance and backlash from conservative segments of society. Some individuals and communities perceive such marriages as a threat to their cultural and social norms. This resistance can manifest in various forms, such as social ostracism, violence, or discrimination against couples and their families. These challenges highlight the need for continued efforts to raise awareness, educate the public, and work towards creating a more inclusive and accepting society.

Conclusion

Love and inter-caste marriages in the Indian subcontinent have profound socioeconomic implications. By challenging caste-based social hierarchies, redefining cultural identity, facilitating economic mobility, bridging economic disparities, promoting social integration, and resisting backward attitudes, these marriages contribute to the broader transformation of society. Recognizing and understanding these implications can help pave the way for a more progressive and inclusive future, where love and personal choice transcend the boundaries of caste, fostering a harmonious and equitable society for all.

Introduction

Love marriages, particularly inter-caste marriages, have gained significant attention in the Indian subcontinent. The union of individuals from different castes and backgrounds is often seen as a symbol of social progress and breaking down traditional barriers. However, navigating the intricate web of family dynamics can pose numerous challenges for couples embarking on this journey. This article explores the complexities, obstacles, and transformations faced by couples in love marriages, with a focus on inter-caste marriages.

Traditional Family Structures and Expectations

In the Indian subcontinent, families play a central role in individuals' lives, and their expectations can heavily influence decisions regarding marriage. Traditional family structures often revolve around notions of caste, religion, and social status. Love marriages disrupt these established norms, as they involve choosing a life partner based on personal compatibility and affection rather than conforming to societal expectations. This clash of ideologies can lead to resistance and conflicts within families, which requires delicate navigation.

Inter-Caste Marriage: Breaking the Barriers

Inter-caste marriages, in particular, challenge deeply ingrained notions of caste hierarchy and social boundaries.

These unions aim to bridge the gaps between different communities and foster inclusivity. However, such marriages are often met with opposition, as they challenge age-old traditions and cultural norms. Families may express concerns about preserving caste purity, maintaining social status, or fear societal backlash. The journey of an inter-caste couple is not just about their individual happiness but also about paving the way for societal change.

Resistance and Conflict

When love marriages are at odds with familial expectations, they can give rise to resistance and conflicts within families. Parents may feel a sense of loss or betrayal, fearing the erosion of family traditions and values. Siblings and extended family members may also express disapproval, influenced by societal pressures. These conflicts can lead to emotional distress, strained relationships, and even estrangement. It is essential for couples to understand the underlying fears and concerns of their families and find ways to address them compassionately.

Bridging the Gap: Communication and Understanding

Building open lines of communication and fostering understanding are vital for bridging the gap between the couple and their families. Couples in love marriages need to initiate and sustain conversations with their families, expressing their emotions, aspirations, and reasons for their choice. This process requires empathy and patience, as family members may need time to come to terms with the new reality. Education and awareness about the benefits of love marriages and inter-caste unions can play a pivotal role in transforming familial perspectives.

The Role of Support Systems

Support systems, such as friends, relatives, or support groups, can provide a crucial anchor for couples facing familial challenges in love marriages. These external networks offer a safe space for sharing experiences, seeking advice, and finding emotional support. Engaging with individuals who have successfully navigated similar circumstances can provide guidance and inspiration. Building a strong support system can empower couples to face difficulties with resilience and maintain their commitment to their relationship.

Shifting Paradigms: Evolution of Family Dynamics

Love marriages, including inter-caste marriages, have the potential to reshape traditional family dynamics. Over time, as families witness the happiness and success of these unions, they may gradually soften their stance and embrace change. New generations within the family can play a vital role in bridging the gap between traditional values and evolving social realities. This transformation can create a ripple effect, inspiring others to question and challenge existing societal norms.

Conclusion

Love marriages, especially inter-caste marriages, bring forth a multitude of challenges rooted in traditional family dynamics. The journey to bridging boundaries is riddled with resistance, conflicts, and emotional turmoil. However, through effective communication, empathy, and building a robust support system, couples can navigate these challenges and foster transformation within their families. Love marriages have the potential to break down barriers, challenge age-old traditions, and pave the way for a more inclusive and harmonious society in the Indian subcontinent. It is through these courageous unions that we can bridge the gap between love and inter-caste marriages, leading to a more progressive future.

Introduction

Inter-caste marriages have emerged as a transformative force in the Indian subcontinent, challenging deep-rooted social hierarchies and reshaping the traditional caste system. These marriages, born out of love and a desire to transcend societal boundaries, have the potential to bridge divides and foster social harmony. This article explores the profound impact of inter-caste marriages on the Indian society, highlighting their role in dismantling age-old prejudices and fostering a more egalitarian future.

The Legacy of the Caste System

The caste system, deeply ingrained in the Indian society for centuries, has perpetuated social stratification and discrimination. It divided people into rigid hierarchical groups, dictating their occupations, social interactions, and even marital choices. This system, with its inherent biases and restrictions, created barriers and perpetuated inequality, making inter-caste marriages a rarity.

Love Transcending Boundaries

Inter-caste marriages are a testament to the power of love, as individuals choose their life partners based on their feelings rather than their caste. Love knows no boundaries, and when two people from different castes decide to unite, they challenge the prevailing norms and forge their own path. Their union becomes a symbol of breaking free from societal constraints and embracing the values of equality and acceptance.

Reshaping Social Hierarchies

Inter-caste marriages have the potential to dismantle traditional social hierarchies. As couples from different castes come together, they challenge the notion of caste-based superiority and inferiority. By disregarding the caste system in their union, they challenge the established order, promoting the idea that love and compatibility are more important than social status or lineage. In doing so, they redefine the parameters of social hierarchy and foster a more inclusive society.

Challenging Prejudices and Stereotypes

One of the most significant impacts of inter-caste marriages is the challenge they pose to deep-seated prejudices and stereotypes. By breaking down barriers and building relationships based on mutual respect, understanding, and love, inter-caste couples challenge the notion that caste determines a person's worth. Their lives and experiences become a living example of how caste should not be a determining factor in judging an individual's character, abilities, or potential.

Promoting Social Integration

Inter-caste marriages act as a powerful catalyst for social integration. They foster interactions and connections between individuals from different castes, facilitating a greater understanding and appreciation of diverse cultures and traditions. As families come together, they bridge the divide between different caste communities, promoting harmony and unity. The children of inter-caste marriages inherit a unique cultural blend, further blurring the lines between castes and strengthening the fabric of a pluralistic society.

Transforming Mindsets

The impact of inter-caste marriages goes beyond the immediate families involved; it extends to the larger society. As more inter-caste marriages occur, societal mindsets begin to evolve. The perception of caste-based differences starts to erode, and people become more accepting of diverse relationships. These marriages serve as a powerful tool to challenge and change societal attitudes, leading to a gradual transformation in how caste is perceived and valued.

Legal and Policy Implications

Over the years, legal and policy frameworks in India have played a crucial role in supporting inter-caste marriages. The Special Marriage Act, 1954, provides a legal framework for inter-caste marriages and protects couples from social backlash and discrimination. Additionally, various state governments have implemented schemes to encourage and financially support inter-caste marriages, recognizing their potential to foster social cohesion.

Overcoming Challenges

Despite the positive impact of inter-caste marriages, they still face challenges and opposition. Deep-rooted societal prejudices, family resistance, and social stigmatization can pose significant hurdles for couples. However, the growing acceptance and changing mindset offer hope for a future where inter-caste marriages are embraced and celebrated.

Conclusion

Inter-caste marriages are reshaping social hierarchies and challenging the caste system, contributing to a more inclusive and egalitarian Indian society. These unions defy traditional boundaries, promote social integration, and serve as a catalyst for transforming mindsets. As the Indian subcontinent continues to witness a rising tide of inter-caste marriages, it is essential to recognize and celebrate their role in bridging boundaries and fostering a more harmonious future for generations to come.

Chapter 11. Love, Honor, and Violence
Addressing Issues of Honor Killings and Violence

Introduction

In the Indian subcontinent, the deeply entrenched social structure and cultural norms often clash with the notion of love and inter-caste marriages. This conflict gives rise to a disturbing phenomenon known as honor killings, where individuals are subjected to violence and even murder in the name of protecting family honor. This article aims to shed light on this grave issue, exploring its underlying causes, consequences, and possible solutions.

Understanding Honor Killings: Culture, Tradition, and Patriarchy

Honor killings are deeply rooted in the cultural fabric of the Indian subcontinent. They stem from a complex interplay of culture, tradition, and patriarchal norms that place family honor above the individual's right to choose their life partner. The practice is often fueled by the fear of diluting caste boundaries and preserving social status, resulting in the suppression of love and the perpetuation of violence.

The Impact of Honor Killings: Lives Lost and Communities Divided

The consequences of honor killings extend far beyond the immediate victims. Families are torn apart, communities become divided, and the very fabric of society is weakened. The loss of lives, particularly those of young individuals seeking to defy societal norms and choose their partners based on love, is a tragic outcome that demands urgent attention.

Breaking the Cycle: Education and Awareness

To address the issue of honor killings, a multifaceted approach is required. Education and awareness play a crucial role in challenging traditional beliefs and norms. By promoting dialogue and creating safe spaces for discussions, we can gradually dismantle the deeply ingrained patriarchal structures that perpetuate violence in the name of honor. Education must emphasize the importance of individual choice, consent, and respect for diverse relationships.

Legal Reforms: Strengthening Justice Systems

Efficient and impartial legal systems are essential in combating honor killings. Governments must enact and enforce stringent laws that explicitly criminalize these acts of violence. Additionally, specialized units within law enforcement agencies should be established to handle honor killing cases sensitively and effectively. By ensuring swift and fair trials, perpetrators can be held accountable, thereby discouraging potential offenders and instilling confidence in the victims and their families.

Support Networks: Empowering Victims and Survivors

Creating robust support networks for victims and survivors is critical to breaking the cycle of violence. NGOs, community organizations, and government agencies should collaborate to provide counseling, legal aid, and safe shelters for those at risk. By offering holistic support, we can empower victims and survivors to rebuild their lives and challenge the social structures that perpetuate violence.

Changing Narratives: Media and Entertainment Industry's Role

The media and entertainment industry possesses significant influence in shaping public opinion and cultural narratives. It is essential for filmmakers, writers, and artists to portray inter-caste marriages and love stories in a positive light, promoting acceptance and breaking stereotypes. By challenging existing narratives and showcasing diverse relationships, they can play a vital role in eroding societal prejudices and promoting inclusivity.

Conclusion

Addressing the issue of honor killings and violence requires a multifaceted approach. By fostering education and awareness, implementing legal reforms, establishing support networks, and changing societal narratives, we can work towards a society that embraces love, honors individual choices, and rejects violence in the name of honor. It is only through collective efforts and a commitment to bridging boundaries that we can create a more inclusive and compassionate future for all.

Chapter 12. Impact on Gender Roles and Gender Equality in Love and Inter-caste Marriages

Introduction

Love and inter-caste marriages have long been a topic of fascination and controversy in the Indian subcontinent. These unions challenge traditional norms and boundaries, often bringing together individuals from different castes, religions, and social backgrounds. While such marriages have the potential to bridge divides and foster social integration, they also have a profound impact on gender roles and gender equality within the relationship and society at large. This article explores the intricate dynamics and consequences of love and inter-caste marriages, shedding light on their transformative influence on gender roles and the pursuit of gender equality.

Rupturing Traditional Gender Roles

Love and inter-caste marriages disrupt the deeply entrenched traditional gender roles prevalent in the Indian subcontinent. These marriages often defy societal expectations, as partners are chosen based on love, compatibility, and personal choices, rather than adhering to caste, religion, or social status. By breaking away from predetermined roles and norms, individuals in such marriages have the opportunity to redefine gender roles within their relationships, promoting equality and shared responsibilities.

Empowering Women

Love and inter-caste marriages have the potential to empower women by granting them agency and autonomy in choosing their life partners. In traditional arranged marriages, women have historically been passive participants, with decisions made on their behalf by family members. However, in love marriages, women often play an active role in selecting their partners, challenging societal norms and expectations. This newfound empowerment can extend beyond marital choices, enabling women to voice their opinions, pursue education and careers, and actively participate in decision-making processes within the relationship.

Challenging Patriarchal Structures

Inter-caste marriages often challenge the patriarchal structures deeply rooted in Indian society. When individuals from different castes come together, they are more likely to question and challenge age-old practices that reinforce gender inequalities. Through open discussions and exposure to different perspectives, inter-caste couples can challenge notions of superiority and inferiority based on gender, thereby dismantling patriarchal beliefs. These marriages serve as catalysts for social change by advocating for gender equality within families and communities.

Navigating Cultural Clashes

Love and inter-caste marriages bring together individuals from diverse cultural backgrounds, each with their own set of customs, traditions, and expectations. This amalgamation of cultures necessitates an ongoing negotiation and redefinition of gender roles. Both partners must navigate and reconcile their respective cultural expectations, leading to a more fluid understanding of gender roles and a gradual dismantling of rigid societal constructs. This process allows for the creation of hybrid identities that embrace the best of both worlds, fostering a sense of inclusivity and acceptance.

Resistance and Backlash

Despite the potential for positive change, love and inter-caste marriages often face resistance and backlash from conservative elements within society. These unions challenge deeply ingrained prejudices, threatening established power structures and social hierarchies. Consequently, couples may encounter societal pressure, discrimination, and even violence. Women, in particular, are more susceptible to facing these challenges, as their decisions to marry outside their caste are often met with greater opposition. However, resilience and collective support can help couples navigate these obstacles and pave the way for a more inclusive and egalitarian society.

Conclusion

Love and inter-caste marriages have a transformative impact on gender roles and gender equality within the Indian subcontinent. By breaking away from traditional norms and defying societal expectations, these unions empower women, challenge patriarchal structures, and foster cultural integration. Despite the challenges and resistance faced, the pursuit of love and inter-caste marriages represents a crucial step towards bridging boundaries and creating a more inclusive and equitable society. By embracing these unions, we can foster a future where gender roles are redefined, and gender equality is no longer an aspiration but a lived reality.

Attitudes and Perspectives on Love and Inter-caste Marriages

Introduction

Love and inter-caste marriages have long been topics of societal debate and discussion in the Indian subcontinent. The cultural, religious, and traditional diversity within the region often leads to a clash of beliefs and values, creating a generation gap in attitudes towards such unions. This article aims to delve into the complexities surrounding inter-caste marriages and explore how the younger and older generations perceive love and relationships, while also highlighting the need to bridge the gap for a more inclusive society.

The Historical Context of Caste and Marriage

To understand the attitudes towards inter-caste marriages, it is crucial to acknowledge the historical significance of the caste system in the Indian subcontinent. Caste divisions have been deeply ingrained in society for centuries, defining social hierarchy, occupation, and even marital alliances. The rigid caste system created barriers to love and intermingling between different castes, reinforcing societal norms and expectations.

The Traditional Perspective on Marriage

Traditionally, marriages in the Indian subcontinent were often arranged, emphasizing the importance of caste compatibility, family status, and economic considerations. Love marriages were relatively rare, and inter-caste marriages were deemed unacceptable due to fears of diluting caste purity and traditions. The older generation largely adhered to these societal norms, prioritizing the preservation of caste identity and lineage.

The Emergence of the Younger Generation

With the advent of modernization, urbanization, and exposure to new ideas through technology and globalization, the younger generation has begun to challenge traditional norms and question the relevance of the caste system in the context of love and marriage. They advocate for the right to choose their partners based on compatibility, love, and personal happiness, rather than adhering to caste constraints.

Changing Attitudes and Perspectives

The younger generation's embrace of inter-caste marriages reflects a shift towards a more inclusive and egalitarian society. They view love as a binding force that transcends societal divisions, valuing emotional connection and shared values over caste identities. They recognize that inter-caste marriages can foster understanding, bridge cultural gaps, and promote social harmony.

Challenges Faced by Inter-caste Couples

Despite the changing attitudes, inter-caste couples often encounter significant challenges in their journey towards acceptance. Social stigma, opposition from families, and community pressure can create immense emotional turmoil. The fear of losing familial support and facing isolation can strain relationships and impact mental well-being. Legal hurdles and discriminatory laws further exacerbate the difficulties faced by inter-caste couples.

Bridging the Generation Gap

Bridging the generation gap on attitudes towards love and inter-caste marriages requires open dialogue, empathy, and education. Encouraging intergenerational conversations can help foster understanding, dispel myths, and challenge deep-rooted biases. Education and awareness campaigns aimed at dispelling caste-based discrimination can play a pivotal role in changing societal perceptions.

The Role of Media and Pop Culture

Media and pop culture have a significant influence on shaping societal attitudes. The portrayal of inter-caste relationships in movies, television shows, and literature can challenge stereotypes and foster acceptance. Highlighting success stories of inter-caste marriages can inspire and encourage others to embrace love beyond caste boundaries.

Legal Reforms and Social Policies

Reforms in legal frameworks and social policies are vital for creating an inclusive society that supports inter-caste marriages. Stricter enforcement of laws prohibiting discrimination based on caste, promoting equal rights and opportunities, and offering legal protection to inter-caste couples can help eliminate obstacles and provide a sense of security.

Building Support Networks

Creating support networks for inter-caste couples can provide them with emotional support, guidance, and resources. Non-governmental organizations, community initiatives, and counseling services can play a crucial role in providing a safe space for couples and helping them navigate the challenges they face.

Conclusion

The generation gap in attitudes towards love and inter-caste marriages is a complex issue rooted in deep-seated cultural beliefs and societal norms. However, the changing perspectives among the younger generation offer hope for a more inclusive and harmonious society. By bridging this gap through education, dialogue, legal reforms, and support networks, we can work towards a future where love and inter-caste marriages are celebrated, and individuals have the freedom to choose their partners based on love and compatibility, rather than caste identities.

Chapter 14. Love Marriages and Inter-caste Marriages in Urban vs. Rural Settings

Introduction

Love and inter-caste marriages have long been a topic of interest and debate in the Indian subcontinent. The social fabric of India is intricately woven with traditions, customs, and deeply rooted caste systems. In recent times, the dynamics of relationships and marriage have been evolving, particularly in urban areas, where the impact of globalization and changing mindsets has challenged traditional norms. This article explores the contrasts and similarities between love marriages and inter-caste marriages in urban and rural settings, shedding light on the challenges, societal perceptions, and the path towards bridging boundaries.

Defining Love Marriages

Love marriages are marriages where the individuals involved choose their life partners based on mutual love, affection, and compatibility. In urban settings, love marriages have become more prevalent, reflecting a shift in societal attitudes and a growing emphasis on individual choice and autonomy. Urban areas provide a conducive environment for couples to meet and interact, leading to greater opportunities for love to blossom.

Love Marriages in Urban Settings

Urban settings offer a diverse and cosmopolitan environment, where people from various backgrounds coexist and interact more frequently. This exposure to different cultures and ideologies broadens the horizons of individuals, enabling them to explore relationships beyond their immediate communities. Urban dwellers often have access to better education, employment prospects, and financial stability, which empower them to make independent choices regarding their partners.

One of the key advantages of love marriages in urban settings is the ability to choose a life partner based on shared interests, values, and compatibility, rather than solely on caste or social status. Love marriages are often seen as a symbol of progress and modernity, as individuals challenge traditional norms and seek personal happiness. However, this shift in mindset is not without its challenges, as societal pressure and family expectations can create obstacles for couples.

Challenges in Urban Love Marriages

While love marriages in urban areas offer more freedom and independence, they are not immune to challenges. Many couples face resistance from their families, who may hold conservative views and adhere to the traditional caste system. Inter-caste love marriages are particularly met with resistance, as they challenge deeply ingrained societal hierarchies and notions of purity.

Social stigma associated with love marriages can lead to ostracization and strained relationships with extended family members and the community. Couples often experience a significant amount of pressure to conform to societal expectations and choose partners within their own caste or community. This can create emotional turmoil, forcing individuals to make difficult choices between their love and familial obligations.

Inter-caste Marriages in Urban Settings

Inter-caste marriages involve individuals from different castes coming together in a sacred union. In urban areas, inter-caste marriages are more likely to occur due to the increased exposure to diverse communities and a wider range of potential partners. The younger generation, influenced by modern ideas of equality and individuality, is more open to breaking caste barriers in their pursuit of love and happiness.

Inter-caste marriages in urban settings can be seen as a form of social mobility, as individuals transcend the limitations imposed by the caste system and create new alliances. Such marriages contribute to the integration and assimilation of different cultures, fostering a sense of unity and diversity within urban communities. However, they are not without their own set of challenges and prejudices.

Challenges in Urban Inter-caste Marriages

Inter-caste marriages often face vehement opposition from conservative sections of society, including families and community members. The notion of "honour" and preserving caste identity can lead to hostility, discrimination, and even violence towards couples daring to challenge the established norms. Couples may also face legal hurdles, as some states in India have laws that restrict inter-caste marriages.

Additionally, the compatibility between individuals from different castes can present its own set of challenges. Differences in lifestyle, cultural practices, and family expectations can create conflicts within the relationship. It requires understanding, compromise, and a willingness to navigate the complexities of merging diverse backgrounds.

Love and Inter-caste Marriages in Rural Settings

Rural areas, in contrast to urban settings, tend to be more rooted in traditional practices and have a stronger adherence to caste-based norms. Love and inter-caste marriages face more significant obstacles in rural communities due to a combination of limited exposure to different cultures, deeply ingrained beliefs, and strong community bonds.

Rural areas often have tightly knit communities where everyone knows each other, making it difficult for individuals to deviate from societal expectations. The fear of ostracization, social boycott, and even violence creates a climate of apprehension for couples contemplating love or inter-caste marriages. In such settings, familial and community approval holds significant weight in the decision-making process.

The Way Forward: Bridging Boundaries

Bridging the divide between love and inter-caste marriages in urban and rural settings requires a multi-faceted approach. Education plays a vital role in challenging social prejudices and stereotypes associated with inter-caste marriages. Awareness campaigns, community dialogues, and sensitization programs can help break down barriers and foster a more inclusive society.

Legal reforms are also crucial to protect the rights of couples and prevent discrimination based on caste or community. State governments must work towards repealing laws that restrict inter-caste marriages and provide support systems for couples facing societal backlash. Alongside legal and educational initiatives, fostering empathy and understanding within families and communities is essential in creating an environment that embraces love and inter-caste marriages.

Conclusion

Love marriages and inter-caste marriages in urban and rural settings in the Indian subcontinent reflect the changing dynamics of relationships and societal norms. While urban areas offer more freedom and opportunities for individuals to choose their life partners, they are not devoid of challenges. Rural settings, on the other hand, present more significant obstacles due to deep-rooted traditions and community expectations.

To bridge the boundaries and create a society that embraces love and inter-caste marriages, it is imperative to address societal prejudices, provide legal protection, and promote awareness and education. By challenging established norms and fostering inclusivity, we can pave the way for a future where love transcends caste, community, and geographical boundaries, leading to a more harmonious and accepting society.

Chapter 15. Media Portrayal and Influence on Love and Inter-caste Marriages

Introduction

Love and inter-caste marriages have long been a subject of fascination and controversy in the Indian subcontinent. These unions challenge deeply ingrained societal norms and boundaries, prompting discussions about identity, tradition, and acceptance. One cannot underestimate the role played by the media in shaping public opinion and influencing attitudes towards these relationships. This article explores the portrayal of love and inter-caste marriages in the media and its impact on society, shedding light on both the positive and negative aspects.

Media Representation and Stereotyping

1. Romanticizing Love: The media often presents love stories as idealized narratives, capturing the hearts of viewers and readers alike. These portrayals transcend caste boundaries, showcasing love as a universal emotion that conquers all obstacles.

2. Reinforcing Stereotypes: However, the media can also perpetuate stereotypes associated with inter-caste marriages. Characters from different castes are often depicted as polar opposites, with tensions and conflicts arising due to societal disapproval. Such portrayals contribute to the existing biases and create barriers to acceptance.

Influence on Public Perception

1. Normalizing Interactions: Through movies, TV shows, and literature, the media has the power to normalize inter-caste interactions and relationships. By showcasing diverse couples and their challenges, it can create a sense of empathy and understanding among viewers.

2. Shaping Attitudes: Media plays a crucial role in shaping public attitudes towards inter-caste marriages. Positive portrayals can challenge deep-rooted prejudices and foster acceptance. On the other hand, negative depictions can reinforce discrimination, fueling social divisions and discouraging individuals from pursuing inter-caste relationships.

Media as a Catalyst for Social Change

1. Challenging Traditions: The media has the potential to challenge traditional norms and pave the way for social progress. By portraying inter-caste marriages as normal and acceptable, it can prompt society to question outdated beliefs and encourage a more inclusive outlook.

2. Creating Awareness: Media platforms provide a powerful medium to educate the masses about the importance of love and inter-caste marriages. They can shed light on the legal and social barriers faced by couples, promoting dialogue and collective action for change.

Responsible Media Representation

1. Promoting Diversity: Media should strive to represent diverse love stories, encompassing various castes, religions, and ethnicities. By showcasing a range of narratives, it can

highlight the richness of human experiences and foster inclusivity.

2. Sensitivity and Authenticity: The media has a responsibility to portray inter-caste relationships with sensitivity and authenticity. Care should be taken to avoid reinforcing stereotypes and instead present nuanced and realistic depictions that resonate with audiences.

Media's Role in Empowering Individuals

1. Inspiring Stories: The media can share inspiring real-life stories of individuals who have successfully navigated inter-caste marriages, overcoming societal obstacles. These narratives can serve as beacons of hope and encouragement for others facing similar challenges.

2. Providing Resources and Support: Media platforms can serve as a valuable resource, providing information, guidance, and support to individuals considering or involved in inter-caste relationships. By connecting people with relevant organizations and communities, the media can create a network of solidarity.

Conclusion

The media's portrayal of love and inter-caste marriages holds immense power to shape public opinion and influence societal attitudes. While it can serve as a catalyst for positive change, it also has the potential to reinforce stereotypes and perpetuate discrimination. Responsible and inclusive media representation is essential for bridging boundaries and fostering acceptance in the Indian subcontinent. By embracing diversity, promoting empathy, and encouraging dialogue, the media can play a

transformative role in dismantling barriers and nurturing a
society that celebrates love in all its forms.

67

Chapter 16. Future Trends and Prospects for Love and Inter-caste Marriages in the Indian Subcontinent

Introduction

Love and inter-caste marriages have always been a subject of great significance in the Indian Subcontinent. Steeped in tradition and cultural norms, the region has witnessed a gradual but noticeable shift in societal attitudes towards these unions. This article explores the future trends and prospects for love and inter-caste marriages in the Indian Subcontinent, shedding light on the changing dynamics and the factors that contribute to this transformation.

Historical Perspective

Love and inter-caste marriages have faced various challenges throughout history due to deep-rooted societal norms and traditions. Caste-based discrimination and the notion of preserving family honor often acted as barriers to these unions. However, with the advent of modernization and globalization, the Indian Subcontinent has been witnessing a gradual shift in perspectives.

Changing Mindsets

One of the significant trends in recent times is the changing mindset of the younger generation. Educated and well-informed individuals are challenging age-old stereotypes and embracing love marriages irrespective of caste. Increased exposure to diverse cultures, educational opportunities, and urbanization has played a pivotal role in shaping this shift.

The Influence of Media

The media has emerged as a powerful catalyst in transforming societal perceptions towards love and inter-caste marriages. Television shows, movies, and web series have started to portray such unions in a positive light, challenging traditional norms. This exposure has contributed to the normalization of inter-caste relationships and has paved the way for broader acceptance.

Rise of Individualism

The rise of individualism has also played a significant role in shaping the future of love and inter-caste marriages. Young adults are now placing more emphasis on personal happiness and fulfillment rather than societal expectations. The desire for autonomy and the freedom to choose one's life partner transcends caste boundaries, leading to a rise in inter-caste marriages.

Economic Factors

Economic factors have had a profound impact on the prospects for inter-caste marriages. With the increasing prominence of the middle class and a growing focus on professional success, individuals are prioritizing compatibility, emotional well-being, and shared aspirations over caste considerations. As financial independence becomes more prevalent, the traditional reliance on caste alliances is slowly diminishing.

Legal Reforms

Legal reforms have been instrumental in providing support and protection to couples involved in inter-caste marriages.

The Special Marriage Act of 1954 in India provides a legal framework for such unions, enabling individuals to marry outside their caste with legal recognition. This legislation has boosted confidence among couples and has contributed to the growth of inter-caste marriages.

Inter-cultural Exchanges

Inter-cultural exchanges and globalization have fostered a greater understanding and appreciation for diverse cultures and traditions. As people interact with individuals from different backgrounds, they develop a broader perspective and are more inclined towards accepting inter-caste relationships. This intermingling of cultures has the potential to break down caste barriers and promote social harmony.

Role of Education

Education has been a driving force behind the changing attitudes towards love and inter-caste marriages. As education levels rise, individuals become more open-minded and are willing to challenge societal norms. Schools and colleges are increasingly emphasizing the importance of equality, diversity, and inclusivity, which helps shape the minds of future generations and encourages them to embrace love without caste barriers.

Conclusion

The Indian Subcontinent is witnessing a remarkable shift in societal attitudes towards love and inter-caste marriages. The future holds promising prospects for these unions, as various factors contribute to the changing dynamics. The younger generation's changing mindset, the influence of media, the rise of individualism, economic factors, legal reforms, inter-cultural exchanges, and the role of education are all playing pivotal roles in shaping a more inclusive and accepting society.

As love triumphs over caste divisions, inter-caste marriages are gradually becoming more accepted and normalized. This transformation signifies a significant departure from traditional norms and reflects a growing emphasis on personal happiness and fulfillment. It is heartening to see individuals challenging age-old stereotypes and prioritizing compatibility and emotional well-being over caste considerations.

Furthermore, legal reforms have provided a legal framework and support for couples involved in inter-caste marriages, boosting their confidence and contributing to the growth of such unions. The influence of media, including television shows, movies, and web series, has also played a crucial role in portraying inter-caste relationships in a positive light, thereby fostering broader acceptance.

Moreover, economic factors and the rise of the middle class have shifted the focus from caste alliances to shared aspirations and compatibility. As financial independence becomes more prevalent, individuals have more agency in choosing their life partners, regardless of caste.

Inter-cultural exchanges and globalization have fostered a greater understanding and appreciation for diverse cultures and traditions, further breaking down caste barriers and promoting social harmony. Education has been instrumental in shaping the mindset of the younger generation, encouraging them to challenge societal norms and embrace love without caste boundaries.

Overall, the future of love and inter-caste marriages in the Indian Subcontinent looks promising. By bridging boundaries and fostering acceptance, society can become more inclusive, harmonious, and respectful of individual choices. As the region continues to evolve and embrace the diversity of love, these unions will contribute to a more vibrant and inclusive society that celebrates love in all its forms.

"Bridging Boundaries: Love and Inter-Caste Marriages in the Indian Subcontinent" is a comprehensive exploration of love and inter-caste marriages in India. This insightful book covers topics such as the historical evolution of marriage patterns, sociocultural influences, legal aspects, socioeconomic implications, family dynamics, and the impact on gender roles. It also examines honor killings, media influence, and the generation gap. Ultimately, the book provides valuable insights and future prospects for love and inter-caste marriages in the Indian Subcontinent, making it a must-read for anyone interested in understanding these complex relationships and promoting social change.

ABOUT THE AUTHOR

Mr. C. P. Kumar is a retired Scientist 'G' from National Institute of Hydrology, Roorkee, Uttarakhand, India. He is also a Reiki Healer and Chakra Balancing practitioner (with pendulum dowsing) and offers Emotional Freedom Technique (EFT) to help individuals with emotional issues. Mr. Kumar has authored many books on technical, spiritual, and social topics.

For further details, you may visit his webpage
https://www.angelfire.com/nh/cpkumar/virgo.html